learn to draw

Cars & Trucks

Learn to draw and color 28 different vehicles, step by easy step, shape by simple shape!

Illustrated by Jeff Shelly

Walter Foster

Getting Started

When you look closely at the drawings in this book, you'll notice that they're made up of basic shapes, such as circles, rectangles, and triangles. To draw all your favorite vehicles, just start with simple shapes as you see here. It's easy and fun!

Circles
are good for drawing many auto features, such as tires and hubcaps.

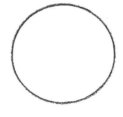 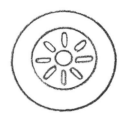

Rectangles
are used to draw the front view of cars, as well as windows and license plates.

Triangles
can make vehicles look fast and sleek.

Coloring Tips

To finish your drawings, you can add color with crayons, markers, or colored pencils. cars and trucks can be almost any color, so bring them to life with lots of fun shades and bright designs!

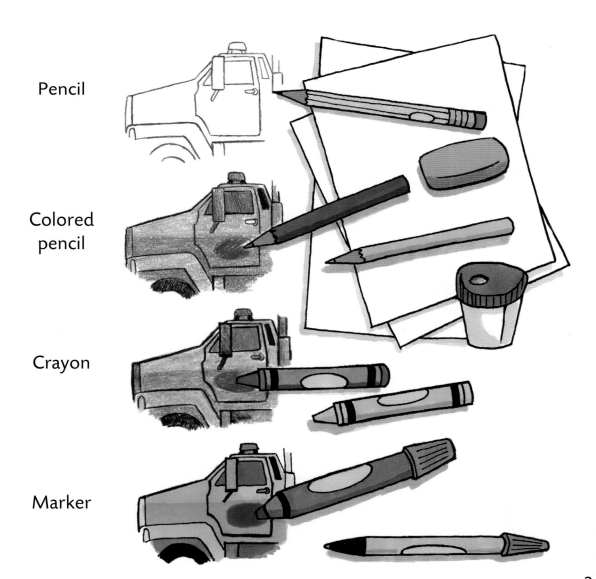

Pencil

Colored pencil

Crayon

Marker

Compact Car

This popular little car is all curves, giving it a fun and bubbly appearance!

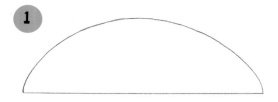

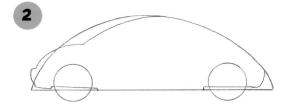

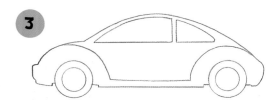

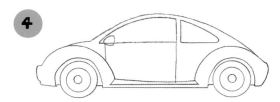

fun fact

Because some European streets are thousands of years old, they aren't always well suited for cars. Small, compact designs are a popular choice for Europeans, but even the tiniest car isn't small enough for some roads—there's a street in Italy that's only 1.5 feet wide!

Euro-Style Car

The flat top, prominent fenders, and two-toned paint job give this sporty car a fashionable, European flair.

Convertible

This sleek and sporty car has a top that folds flat, so you can use a simple rectangle for a speedy start!

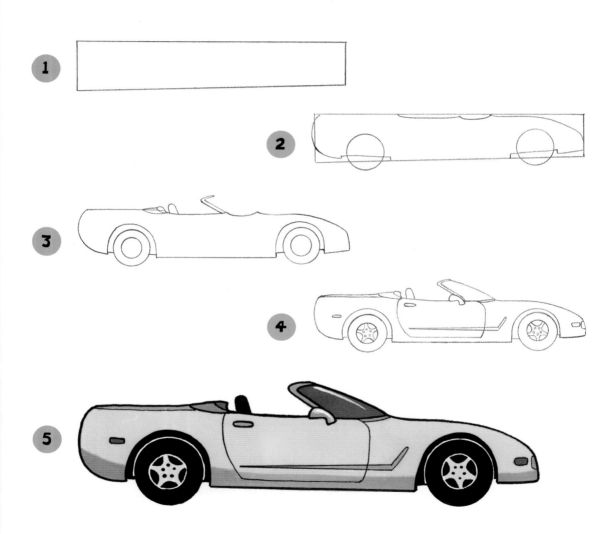

fun fact

The first "power top" convertible was introduced in 1939, starting an open-air craze that lasted 30 years. But automakers retired these cars in the '70s because of new regulations and safety concerns. The cars returned with improvements in 1982.

Armored Truck

To draw this strong and sturdy "safe on wheels,"
begin with simple circles, rectangles, and
squares—all the basic shapes!

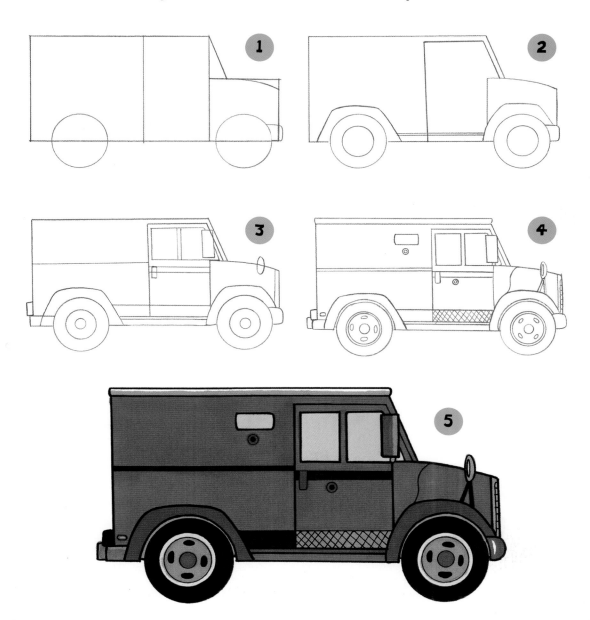

Ambulance

When you color this emergency vehicle,
use bright colors so it really stands out when
it screams down the road.

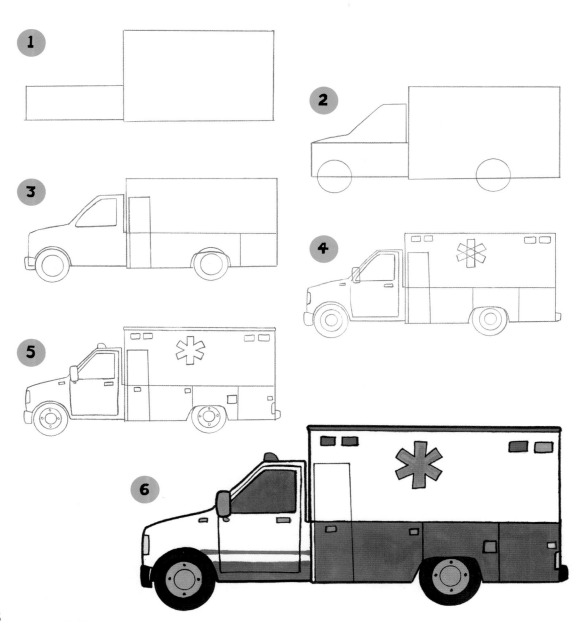

Passenger SUV

This durable sport utility vehicle can carry all your cargo, making it a mobile home-away-from home!

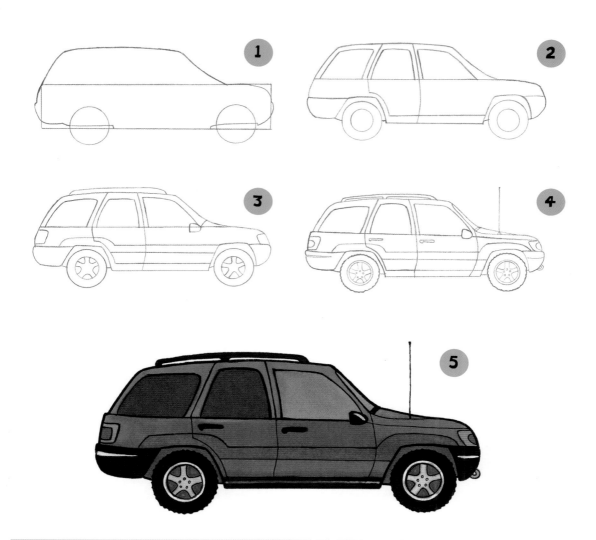

fun fact

In 1940, during World War II, the U.S. Army needed a large, sturdy passenger vehicle for scouting out missions. As a result, the Army developed the earliest form of the sports utility vehicle.

Police Car

Patrol cars are easy to identify.
This one's white and dark markings follow
a distinct, law-abiding pattern.

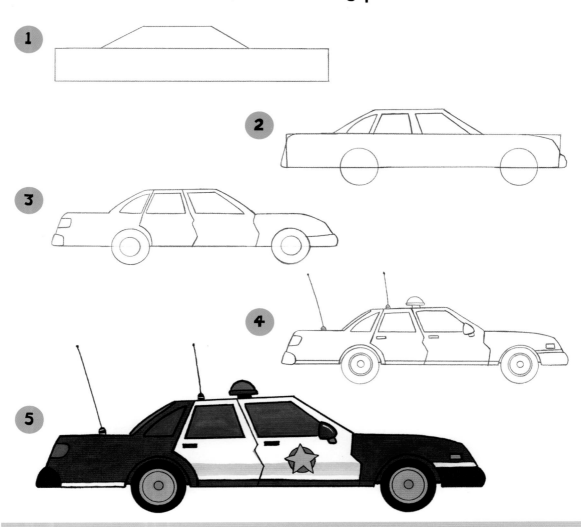

fun fact

Many police cars are equipped with a switch that
turns off all the interior lights and dims the outside lights,
allowing them to shift quickly into stealth mode!

Ice Cream Truck

The tall, boxy shape of this truck shouts ice cream! Use super-bright colors and draw your favorite frozen treats!

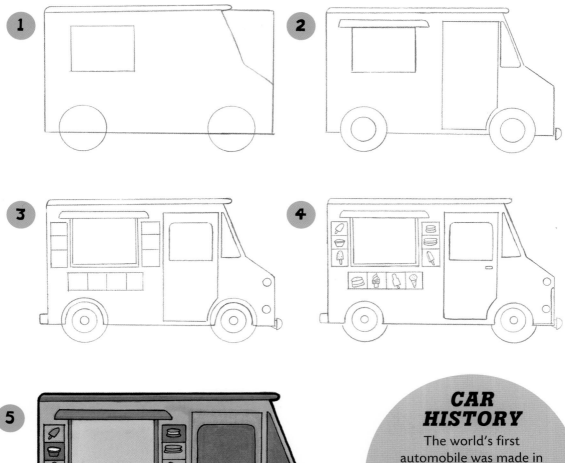

CAR HISTORY

The world's first automobile was made in France in 1871 by Nicolas Cugnot. Powered by a two-cylinder steam engine, its top speed was 2.3 mph—walking speed is 3 mph!

Dually Truck

This tough vehicle has four rear wheels, giving it extra weight-bearing power for carrying heavy loads in its bed.

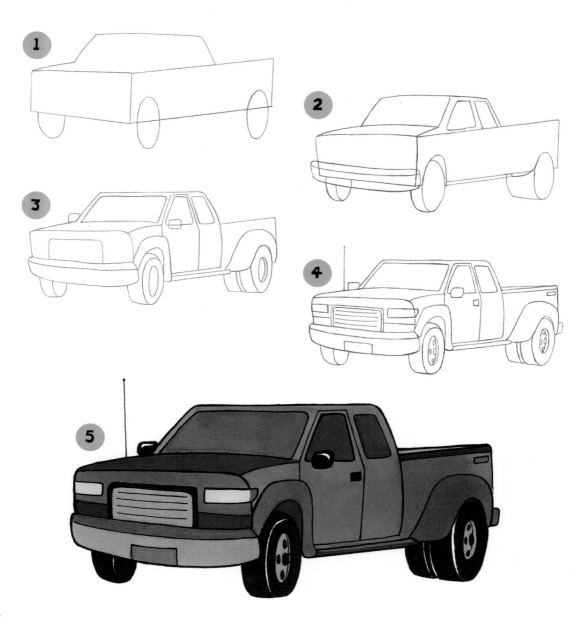

Extreme ATV

This rugged and angular truck goes
all-terrain. It can trek over any type of land—
sand, swamp, or stone!

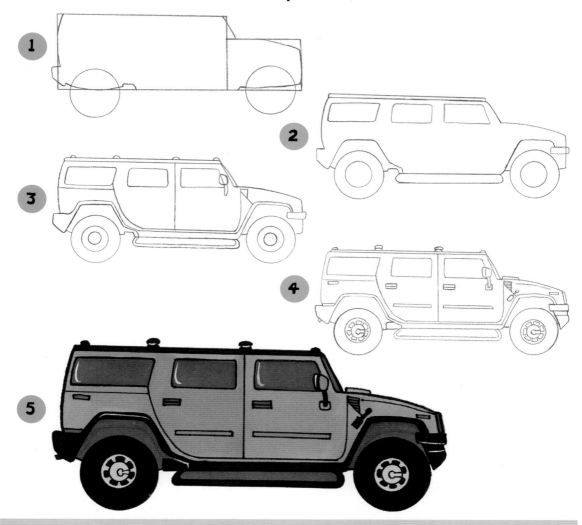

fun fact

Despite their bulky appearance, these ATVs are actually
lightweight vehicles that can be lifted and moved by
helicopter cables. They were even designed so they could be
dropped from the sky with a parachute!

Dune Buggy

Built for conquering steep sand dunes, this vehicle has "roll bars" behind the seats to protect passengers if the buggy flips.

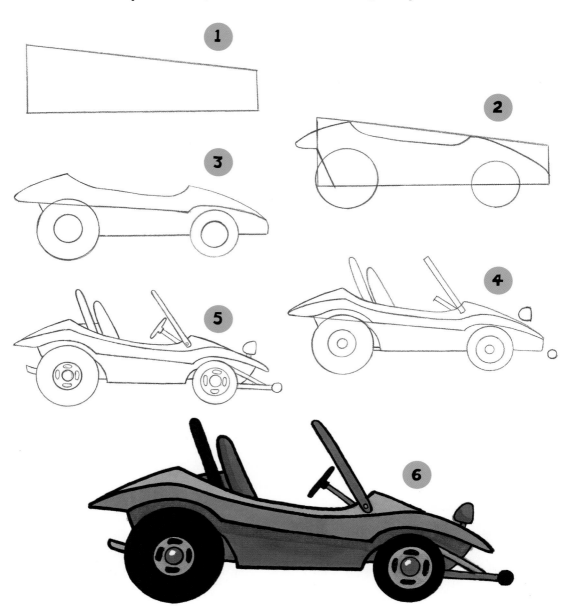

Stock Racecar

The back of this car sports a spoiler—
an upward swoop at the tip—to keep the rear end
from lifting at high speeds!

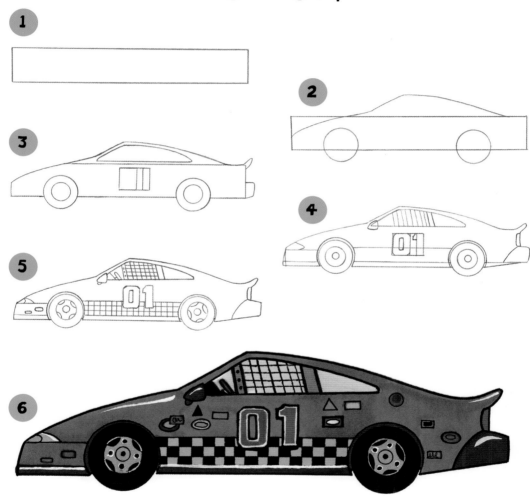

Drag Racecar

This hot rod is shaped like a thin arrowhead, so it can cut through the air and accelerate with amazing speed!

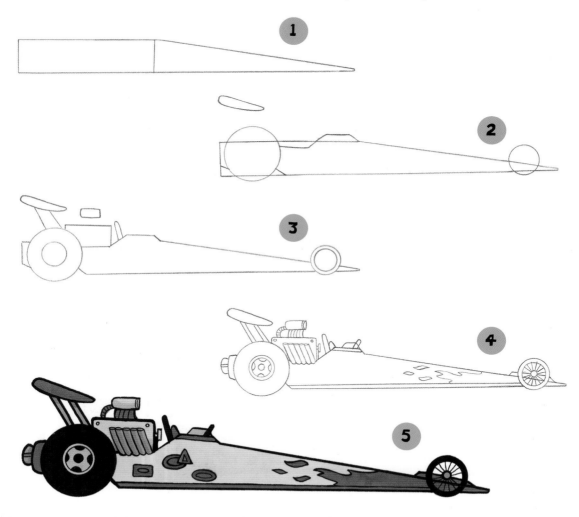

fun fact

Drag racecars can hit speeds of more than 300 miles per hour in just 5 seconds! It's no wonder that these incredibly fast machines need to use parachutes to slow down.

Horse Trailer

This pickup truck hauls precious cargo—horses!
Make the trailer tall enough for its
four-legged passengers.

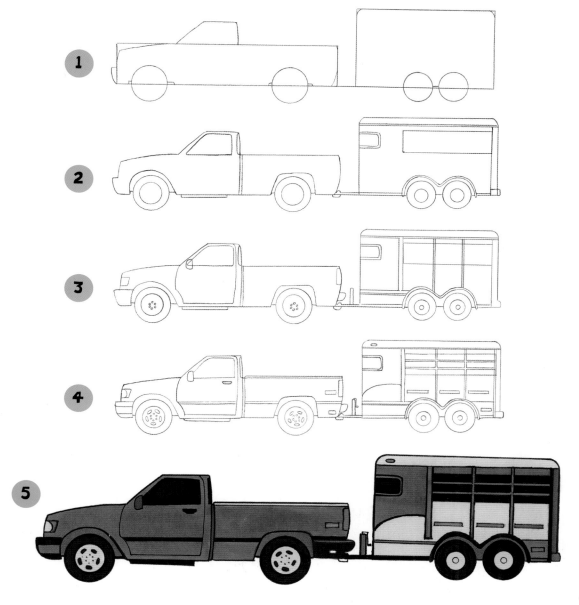

School Bus

The long body of this yellow "limousine" allows for plenty of seats—some buses can carry more than 80 kids at a time!

fun fact

All school buses have been painted yellow since 1939 when representatives from all 48 states agreed it was easiest to see black lettering against yellow.

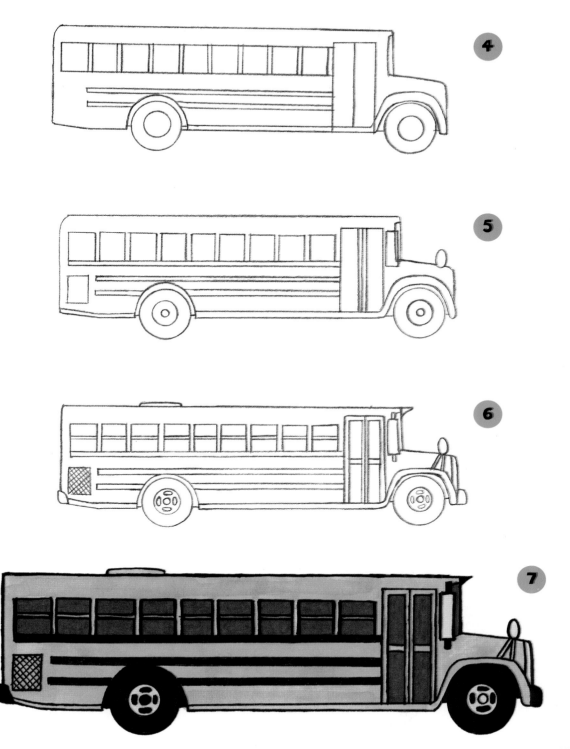

4

5

6

7

Futuristic Car

Prototype cars like this one show what future cars might look like. Styles change all the time, and this ground-hugging sports car may be a glimpse of what's to come!

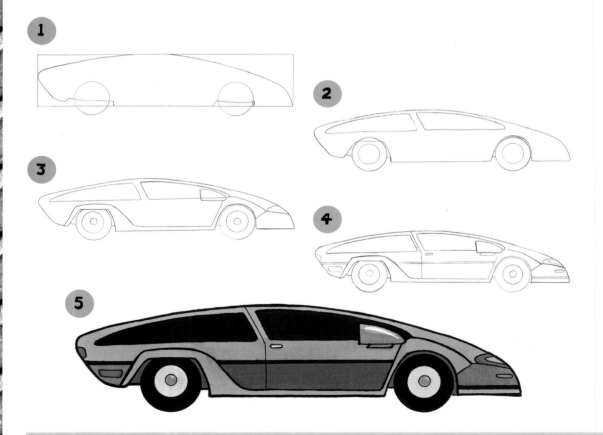

1

2

3

4

5

SWAT Van

This tall, squarish van transports all the protective gear that a SWAT team needs to face any dangerous situation.

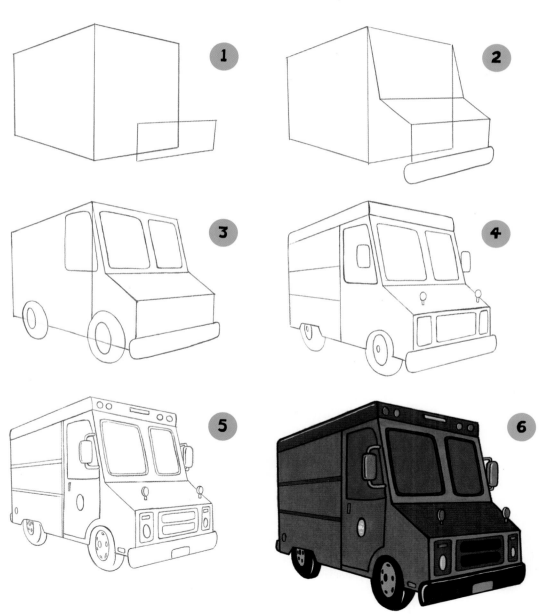

Lifeguard SUV

Aside from the windshield, this open-air sport utility vehicle has no windows or roof, making it perfect for cruising the beach!

fun fact

Most SUVs have 4-wheel drive, that is each of the four wheels is powered to move and turn. This feature makes getting stuck in the sand less likely because it supplies the vehicle with more power and traction.

Stretch Limousine

The long, roomy limousine allows people to ride in luxury. With TVS, chauffeurs, and more, these cars make you feel like a star!

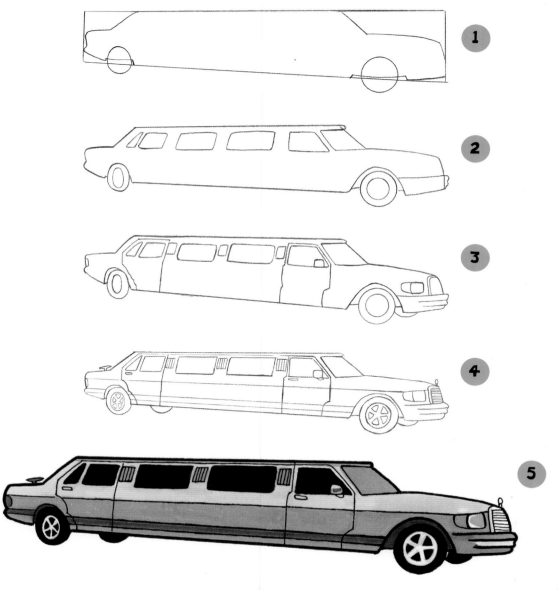

23

Monster Truck

This tall truck has giant wheels that allow it to crawl over humongous obstacles—including piles of other cars!

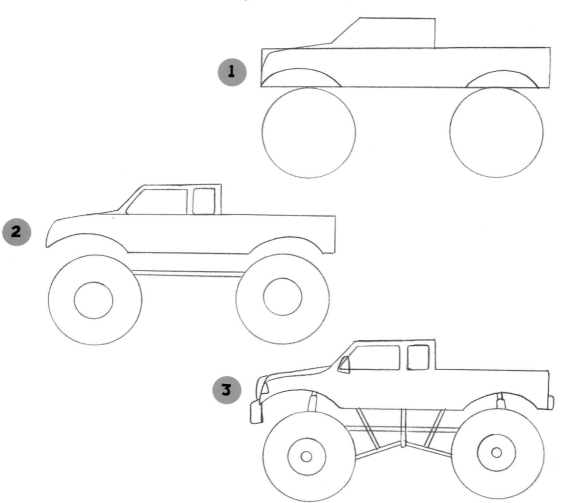

fun fact   The enormous tires used to create monster trucks are even bigger than you might imagine—each tire is usually more than 60 inches tall and 40 inches wide.

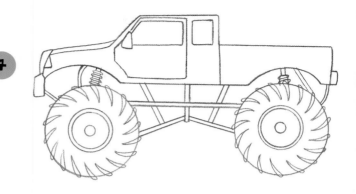

4

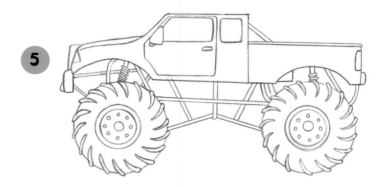

5

6

Recycling Truck

These hi-tech trucks make the driver's job easier—they have "arms" that lift and dump recyclables into their own compartment!

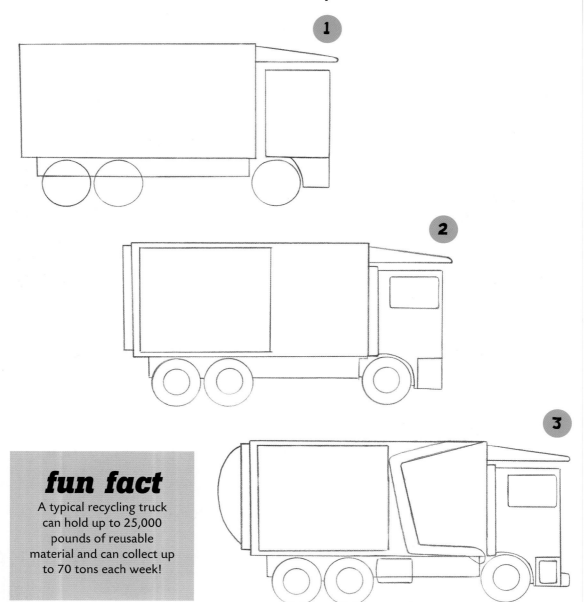

fun fact
A typical recycling truck can hold up to 25,000 pounds of reusable material and can collect up to 70 tons each week!

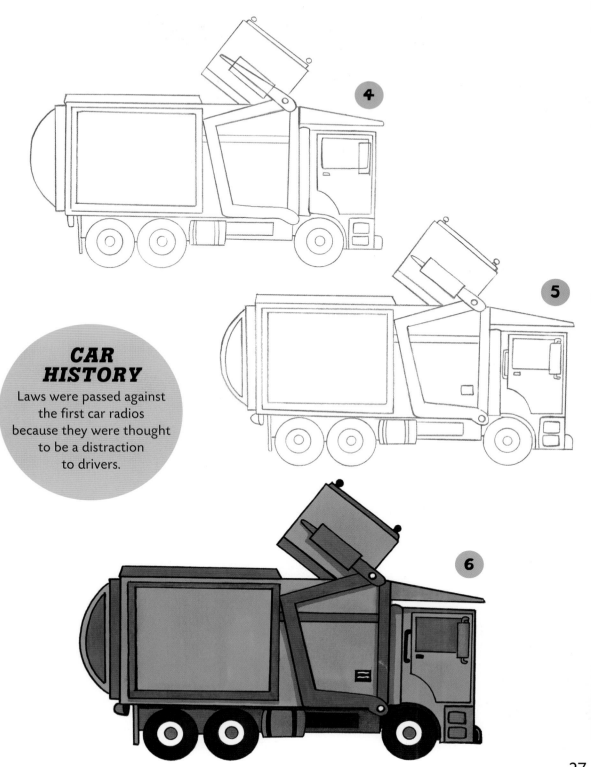

CAR HISTORY

Laws were passed against the first car radios because they were thought to be a distraction to drivers.

4

5

6

Dump Truck

This powerful vehicle has a broad, deep bed that holds heavy loads, so the truck needs very large wheels and a solid frame.

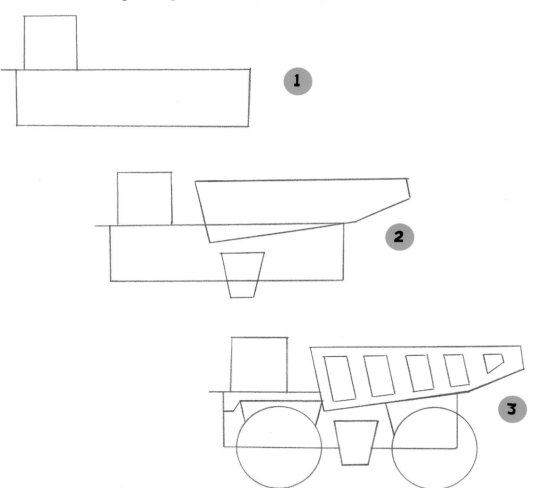

4

5

6

7

Tow Truck

Draw this crane-bearing service vehicle with a large cab and plenty of compartments for storing towing tools.

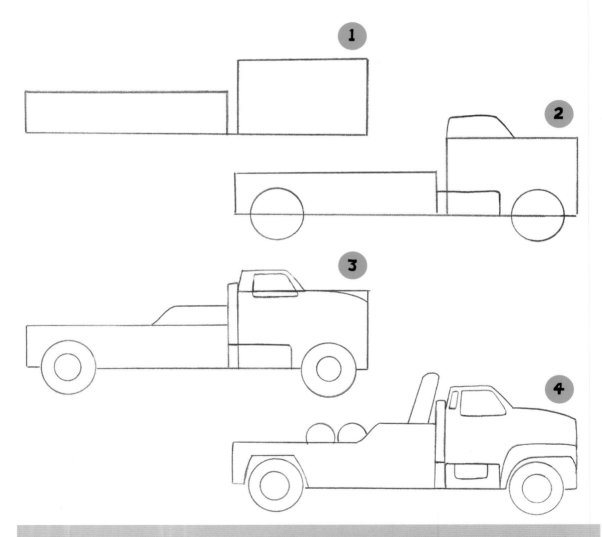

fun fact

Heavy-duty tow trucks can haul loads that weigh up to 45,000 pounds—their cargo can include buses, other big trucks, or even buildings!

Street Sweeper

The large, round, spinning brush attached to one side of this sweeper prevents debris from clogging up gutters and drains.

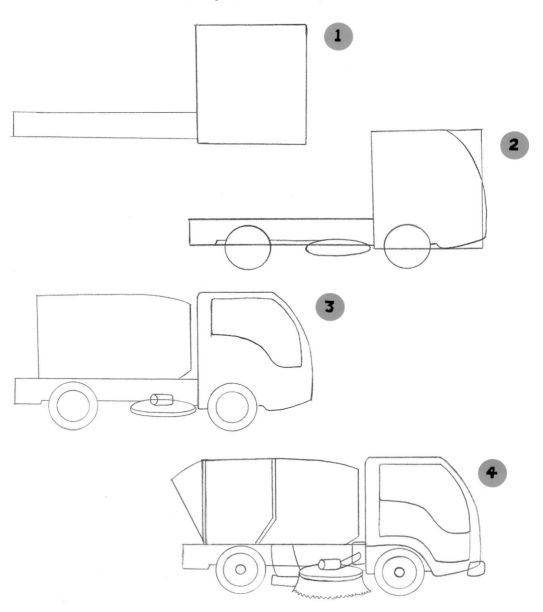

5

6

7

fun fact

In 1896, Charles Brooks patented new ideas that, when combined, led to a dual-purpose street sweeper truck. In this original design, the front fender sported revolving brushes that could be replaced with scrapers during snowy winters.

Snowplow

This helpful truck has a scoop attached to the front that pushes snow from its path, clearing the streets faster than you can shovel!

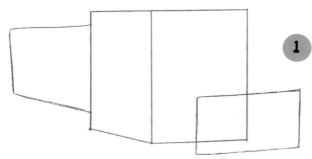

1

fun fact

The first motor-driven snowplow in the United States appeared in Michigan in the 1920s. The vehicle was simply a truck with wooden wings attached to the running boards!

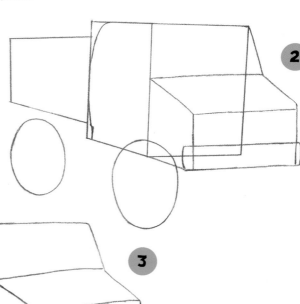

2

3

4

5

6

Cement Truck

The barrel of this construction truck rotates to keep the cement mixture inside from becoming a solid mass of concrete!

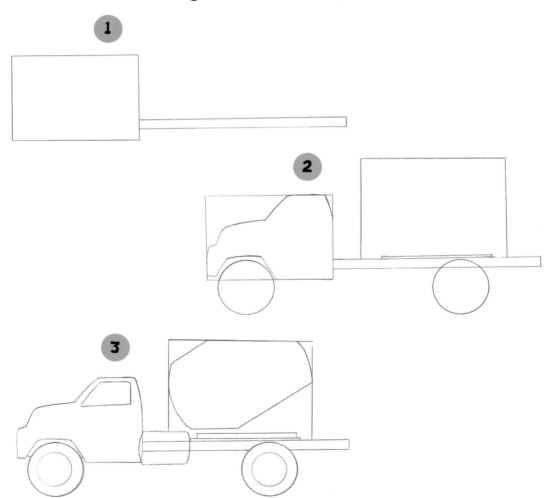

1

2

3

fun fact

The inside of the mixing barrel is wrapped with fins that are arranged in a spiral formation; spinning the drum in one direction will mix the cement, and spinning it the other way will guide the wet cement out of the barrel!

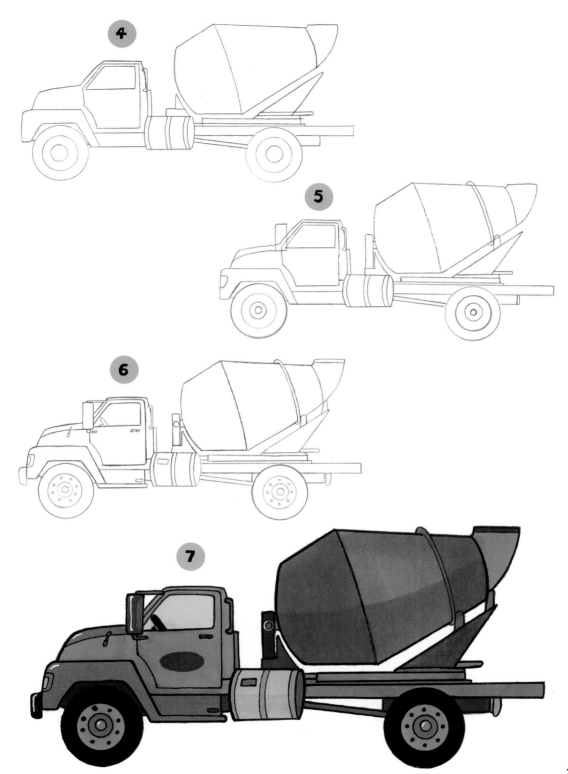

Fire Engine

When the sirens are blaring on this bright red truck, all cars and trucks make room for this blaze-fighting machine.

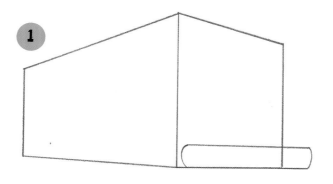

fun fact

Before there were fire trucks, people fought fires with hand-held buckets of water. But fire departments have come a long way. Pumper trucks, like the one you see here, can pump out more than 1,200 gallons of water a minute!

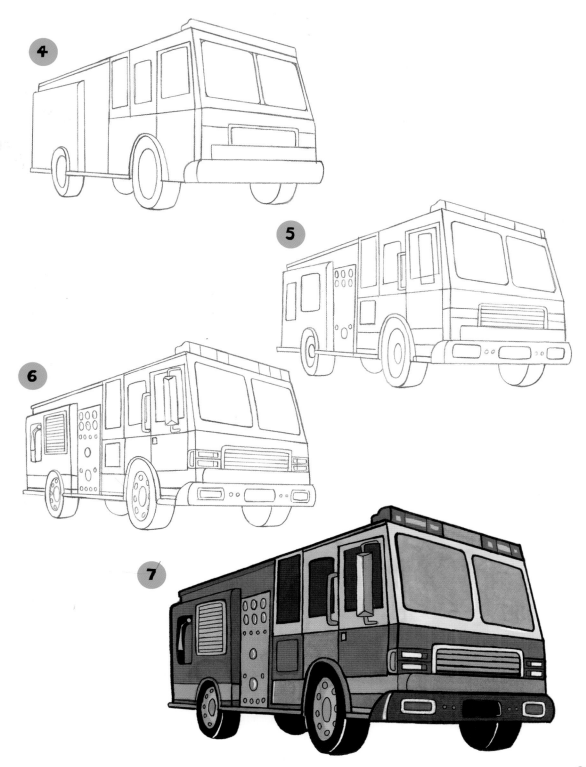

Sports Car

This hot, low-to-the-ground car has a slick, curved shape that allows it to turn corners with speed and ease.

1

2

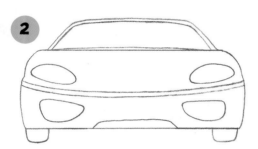

3

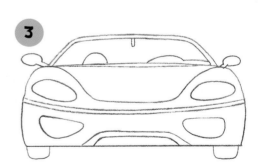

4

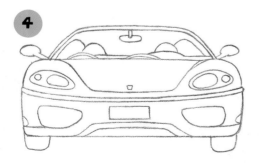

5